Principles of STATISTICS

DANTES/DSST* Test Study Guide

All rights reserved. This Study Guide, Book and Flashcards are protected under the US Copyright Law. No part of this book or study guide or flashcards may be reproduced, distributed or stored in a retrieval system, or transmitted in any form or by any means, electronic, mechanical, photocopying, recording, or otherwise, without the prior written permission of the publisher Breely Crush Publishing, LLC.

© 2026 Breely Crush Publishing, LLC

DSST is a registered trademark of The Thomson Corporation and its affiliated companies, and does not endorse this book.

971010822143

Copyright ©2003 - 2026, Breely Crush Publishing, LLC.

All rights reserved.

This Study Guide, Book and Flashcards are protected under the US Copyright Law. No part of this publication may be reproduced, distributed or stored in a retrieval system, or transmitted in any form or by any means, electronic, mechanical, photocopying, recording, or otherwise, without the prior written permission of the publisher Breely Crush Publishing, LLC.

Published by Breely Crush Publishing, LLC
10808 River Front Parkway
South Jordan, UT 84095
www.breelycrushpublishing.com

ISBN-10: 1-61433-686-5
ISBN-13: 978-1-61433-686-0

Printed and bound in the United States of America.

DSST is a registered trademark of The Thomson Corporation and its affiliated companies, and does not endorse this book.

Table of Contents

Descriptive Statistics *1*
Sampling/Experimenting Methods and Terms *2*
Histograms *4*
Quartiles *5*
Box Plots *6*
Stem and Leaf Plots *8*
Mean *9*
Standard Deviation *10*
Probability *11*
Conditional Probability *12*
Simple Probability *14*
Z Scores *16*
Empirical Rule *19*
Correlation and Regression *20*
Scatter Diagram *22*
Positive Linear Correlation *22*
Negative Linear Correlation *23*
Correlation Coefficient *24*
Linear Regression *24*
Permutations *25*
Combinations *26*
Binomial Formula *26*
Discrete and Continuous Random Variables *27*
Chance Models and Sampling *29*
Sampling Distributions *30*
Confidence Intervals *31*
Tests of Significance *34*
Comparing Sample Means *36*
Sample Questions *42*
Answer Key *68*
Test Taking Strategies *69*
Legal Note *70*

Descriptive Statistics

What are statistics? Statistics allows you to organize, evaluate, and interpret data. Data can be analyzed through calculations as well as graphs.

What is "inductive statistics"? Inductive statistics are statistics that enable you to make conclusions and decisions based on data.

What is "descriptive statistics"? Descriptive statistics do NOT make conclusions or inferences based on the data. Descriptive statistics are meant to describe and analyze a group without making a decision.

What are variables? A variable is a characteristic which describes an individual. For example, for a statistician studying the distribution of test scores in a certain population the score each individual received on the test would be the variable. The key to a good experiment is that the number of variables is minimized. For example, the students taking the test likely all studied for different amounts of time, slept for different amounts of time, and ate at different times. These are all also variables.

What is a quantitative variable? A quantitative variable is a variable which can be expressed in terms of a numerical value. Height, weight, scores on a test, year in school and age are all examples of quantitative variables.

What is a qualitative variable? A qualitative variable is a variable which cannot be expressed in terms of a numerical value. Qualitative variables are described in terms of category, and for this reason they are also called categorical values. Skin color, eye color, gender, ethnicity, and favorite restaurant are all examples of qualitative variables.

What are explanatory and response variables? A response variable is the variable which is influenced by the other variable. They are sometimes referred to as dependent variables. An explanatory variable is the variable which it is believed explains the change in a response variable. Explanatory variables are sometimes referred to as independent variables. When graphing, the explanatory variable is graphed along the x axis, and the response variable is graphed along the y axis.

 Sampling/Experimenting Methods and Terms

What is the difference between a sample and population? A population is the group which a study or experiment is meant to determine information about. A sample is a group within a population which is used to determine information about the population.

What are samples and experiments? There are two different ways of producing or collecting data. They are observational studies and experimentation. A study consists of observing individuals and collecting data, but not influencing the individuals, or subjects, in any way. Observational studies are done using sample populations to draw conclusions. An experiment consists of imposing a treatment on an individual or group and observing the response to it.

What types of samples are there? To understand samples, it is important to know the difference between a sample and a census. A sample takes a portion of the population being studied and gathers information about it. A census gathers information about every individual in a sample. Convenience samples consist of sampling the people who are easiest to reach, and voluntary response samples are samples in which the participants choose themselves. These two types of samples are generally highly biased, and do not yield accurate results. The more random a sample is, the less biased the results will be. There are three general types of random samples, and they are simple random samples, stratified random samples, and cluster samples.

What are simple random samples? In a simple random sample (SRS) the participants are chosen out of the population so that every individual has an equal chance of being chosen.

> **Example of simple random sample:** An employer wishes to conduct a drug test on his employees, but does not want to go to the trouble of testing all of them. He assigns each employee a number, each with the same probability of being chosen, and has his computer randomly select ten percent of his employees to be tested. This is a simple random sample because every member of the population being studied, or all of the employees, had the same chance of being chosen.

What are stratified random samples? In a stratified random sample, the population is divided in to groups with important similarities. These groups are called strata. An SRS is conducted in each separate strata.

> **Example of stratified random sample:** A gym teacher needs to determine the average strength of his students, but does have the time to test every one of them individually. He divides the class into boys and girls, assigns them each a number,

and has his computer randomly select a number of students from each group. This would be a stratified random sample because the class was split into two strata, boys and girls, and then an SRS is conducted from there.

What are cluster samples? In a cluster sample the population is divided into clusters. Then a random sample of clusters is chosen, and all of the members of each cluster participate.

> **Example of cluster sample:** A teacher has split her class into groups of three to work on a large project. The day the project was due she ran out of time in class for all of the students to present, and decides to randomly select groups to present, and to give the whole class a grade based on the preparedness of the randomly chosen groups. This is a cluster sample because the class was divided into clusters, which are the project groups, and the whole class is being given a grade based on the individuals in the chosen groups. In other words, a conclusion about the population is being determined based on the individuals in the clusters.

What is important in an experiment? The point of an experiment is to measure the effect of a treatment, so it is important to have a control which does not receive the treatment for comparison. It is also important to have a large number of subjects to test, so that individual variables don't corrupt the conclusions. Randomization is also vital. The process of determining which subjects receive which treatment, if any, must be a random process.

What is block design? Block design refers to a type of experiment which divides subjects into predetermined groups, which are known or suspected to affect the results. Then groups within each block are assigned the different treatments. For example, a test for an energy drink may split subjects up by gender.

What is matched pairs design? In matched pairs design experimental subjects are matched in pairs so that two similar subjects are paired with each other, and each given a different treatment.

What is a double blind experiment? A double blind experiment is a experiment in which the subjects do not know what treatment they are receiving, and the people administering the treatment do not know which patients are receiving which treatments either. This removes effects such as experimenter bias and the placebo effect.

Histograms

What are histograms? Histograms are a type of frequency distribution. Frequency distributions allow you to categorize a vast amount of data. Each category will have a specific frequency which is the number of data in that category.

There are terms you need to be familiar with regarding frequency distributions:

1. Class Interval: The class interval is the upper and lower limit for each category.
2. Size of Interval: The size of the interval is determined by finding the difference between the upper and lower limit for the category.
3. Class Mark: The class mark is located at the midpoint of the class interval. You can find this midpoint by adding the upper and lower limits and dividing by 2.

Histograms are composed of a set of **rectangles** that have:

1. Bases on the *X*-axis
2. Centers at the class marks
3. Lengths equal to the class interval sizes
4. Areas proportional to the class frequencies

Following is an example of when you could create a histogram.

Thomas Jefferson Middle School is having a reading competition. Students recorded the number of books they read in the month of October.

Number of Students	Number of Books Read
2	0
7	4
8	8
18	12
7	16
4	20
1	24

Following is a Histogram based on this data:

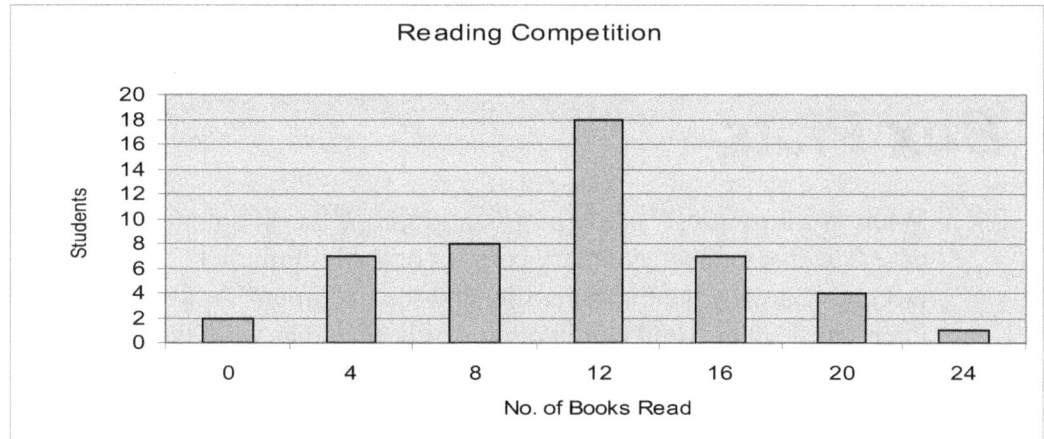

Quartiles

What are quartiles? Quartiles represent different components of the data set.

- The lower quartile (LQ) is a number such that at least 25% of the numbers in the data set are no larger than this number.

- The second quartile is the median. The Median is the middle value or the arithmetic mean of the middle values. The following example will demonstrate how to find the Median.

  Sample Data = {3, 3, 5, 6, 7, 9, 10, 12, 14}

  The Median = 7 because it has four numbers to the left of it and four numbers to the right of it in the sample data.

  NOTE: The data MUST be in numerical order to find the Median. For example, if you are given a sample data set of {5, 6, 12, 3, 3, 10, 7, 14, 9} you must first put it in numerical order: {3, 3, 5, 6, 7, 9, 10, 12, 14} to find the correct Median of 7.

- The upper quartile (UQ) is a number such that at least 75% of the numbers in the data set are no larger than this number.

What is the "normal approximation for data"? Normal approximation for data refers to approximating data in a histogram based on the normal curve if the data values are converted to standard units. In other words, the area under the histogram over various regions is approximately equal to the area of the normal curve over the same regions.

Box Plots

What is a box plot? A box plot is a graph of the five number summary of a set of data. The five number summary consists of the minimum, the first quartile, the median (second quartile), the third quartile, and the maximum. A box is used to represent the interquartile range (IQR), or in other words, the range from the first quartile to the third quartile. There is a line dividing the box where the median is located, and lines extend from the box to the minimum and maximum of the data set. Box plots can be drawn either vertically or horizontally.

Example: A company wishes to know if one of their products is popular or if they should stop making it. They take a random poll of 20 people in which they asks the subjects to rate their opinion of the product on a scale of 1-10. The results are shown below.

5	6	9	8	4	6	8	5	5	9
6	7	7	9	6	5	6	8	5	8

The company uses the data to calculate the five number summary for the data.

Min: 4   Q1: 5   Med: 6   Q3: 8   Max: 9

The box plot for this data is shown below.

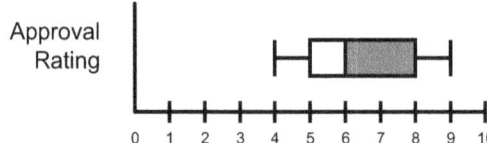

What are box plots used for? A box plot is one of the less detailed types of graphs, and because of this the method is most useful when comparing different data sets.

Example: The same company has decided that they are going to drop one of their products. They narrow it down to the one described above and two others. The take a new random sample of 100 people and ask them to rate their opinions of the 3 products on a scale of 1-10.

	Min:	Q1:	Med:	Q3:	Max
Product 1:	4	5	6	8	9
Product 2:	3	6	6.5	7	8
Product 3:	1	2	5	9	10

The data is put into a box plot for comparison.

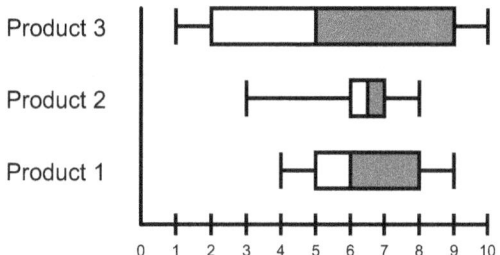

Box plots can be a fast and easy way of comparing the spread, range, and medians of different sets of data.

What about outliers? When the 1.5 X IQR confirms that a data point is an outlier, it is removed from the data set, and is instead represented by a mark on the graph. When outliers are graphed on a box plot like this, it is called a modified box plot.

Example: A second company which in competition with the first company notices that they have withdrawn a product, and decides to have a poll of their own. They take a random sample of 10 people, and ask them to rate the product on a scale from 1-10. Their poll yields the following result.

8	7	9	6	7	8	9	10	2	7

Then calculate the five number summary for the data:

Min: 2 Q1: 6.5 Med: 7.5 Q3: 8.5 Max: 10

The company believes the value of 2 to be an outlier, and they confirm using the IQR x 1.5 Rule.

$1.5 \times IQR = 1.5 \times (8.5-6.50) = 1.5 \times 2 = 3$

Q3 + 3 = 11.5 Therefore there are no outliers above the third quartile.
Q1 - 3 = 3.5 Therefore, because 2 is less than 3.5, it is an outlier.

The modified box plot of the data set is shown below.

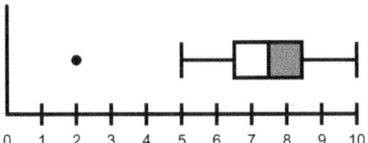

Stem and Leaf Plots

What is a stem plot? A stem plot, or stem and leaf plot, is a type of display method for single variable analysis. They are formed by first ordering each value into a stem portion and a leaf portion. The leaf portion includes the final digit, and the stem portion includes everything but the final digit. Then, the stem values are written in a vertical column, with smallest at the top, and lowest at the bottom, and a vertical line in drawn to the right of the numbers. Finally, the leaf values are written horizontally across from their corresponding stem values, in increasing order from the left to right.

Example: A teacher wishes to display for her students the distribution of grades on the last test. To do this she uses a stem plot so that each student can see their score in relation to the rest of the class. The scores of the class are shown below.

88	64	59	20	77
46	86	98	100	87
87	88	95	72	73
65	85	99	84	86
85	75	83	85	78
65	54	64	88	77

For this data, the stem will represent the tens place value, and the leaf will represent the ones place value.

```
 1 |
 2 | 0
 3 |
 4 | 6
 5 | 4 9
 6 | 4 4 5 5
 7 | 2 3 5 7 7 8
 8 | 3 4 5 5 5 6 6 7 7 8
 9 | 4 5 8 9 9
10 | 0
```

What are stem plots used for? A stem plot is used as a quick method of displaying the general shape of the data, while still incorporating the actual numerical values. Because numerical values are used, the variable must be quantitative. Stem plots do not work well for large data sets, or for sets in which the variable contains many decimal places. There are two ways a stem plot can be modified. They are by splitting stems, which is cutting the stem into two parts, and by trimming, which is eliminating one decimal place at the end of each value.

Mean

How do you find the "Mean" from sample data? The "Mean" is also referred to as the "Arithmetic Mean".

The Arithmetic Mean is calculated by finding the **sum** of all "N" values and dividing by N. This is the general formula to calculate the arithmetic mean: $\frac{\sum_{i=1}^{n} X_i}{N}$

Example of Arithmetic Mean:

What is the arithmetic mean of the numbers 10, 8, 6, 12, and 9?

$X = (10 + 8 + 6 + 12 + 9) = 45$ and $N = 5$ because there 5 numbers in the list.

Therefore, $\frac{45}{5} = \frac{9}{1} = \mathbf{9}$

Standard Deviation

What is "Standard Deviation"? Standard Deviation relates data points to the Mean of the sample data set. Simply put, it is the average amount away from the mean the data points are. Standard Deviation is a measure of spread. It is represented by either s or σ.

Standard Deviation (s) is calculated using: $s = \sqrt{\dfrac{\sum_{i=1}^{n}(X_i - \bar{X})^2}{N}}$

Where $\bar{X}$ = the Arithmetic Mean of the data set

X_i = the value of each number in the data set

N = Number of values in the data set

Example of Standard Deviation: Find the Standard Deviation of the following set of numbers: {12, 6, 7, 3, 15, 10, 18, 5}.

$$\bar{X} = \frac{12 - 6 + 7 - 3 - 15 - 10 + 18 + 5}{8} = \frac{76}{8} = 9.5$$

$$s = \sqrt{\frac{(12-9.5)^2 + (6-9.5)^2 + (7-9.5)^2 + (3-9.5)^2 + (15-9.5)^2 + (10-9.5)^2 + (18-9.5)^2 + (5-9.5)^2}{8}}$$

Therefore, $s = \sqrt{23.75} = 4.87$

What is variance? You may have noticed that the equation for standard deviation is square rooted. Without this square root it is variance that is determined, not standard deviation. Therefore, variance can be used as another description of spread. The higher the spread of a set of data, the higher the variance will be. Variance is generally only used in determining standard deviation. It is signified by s^2 or σ^2 as the case may be.

Probability

What is probability? Probability is defined as the likelihood that an event will occur expressed as the ratio of the number of favorable outcomes in the set of outcomes divided by the total number of possible outcomes.

What are outcomes and events? An outcome is the result of an experiment or other situation involving uncertainty. An event is a collection of outcomes.

For example, let's say you toss a coin. What is the probability that the outcome will be a "Head"? There are two possible outcomes which are "Head" or "Tail". Therefore, the probability is ½.

What are the basic rules of probability? Probability is denoted with **P(event)**. Probability is written in terms of the probability that a specific "event" will occur. For example, to determine the probability that event A will occur you denote this as **P(A).**

NOTE: The value of P **must** be between 0 and 1. Therefore, $0 \leq P(A) \leq 1$.

This means that the probability that event A will NOT occur is denoted as P(Not A) = 1- P(A).

How do you find the probability of a simple event? A simple event consists of finding the probability of one event "A". For example, event "A" can be rolling a die once and having an outcome of the number 3.

Find the probability of rolling a "3" when you throw one die.

P(event) = $\frac{\text{number of possible occurrences in one trail}}{\text{number of possible outcomes in sample space}}$

P(3) = $\frac{\text{number of 3's on die}}{\text{Total number of numbers on die}}$ = $\frac{1}{6}$

Conversely, find the probability that you don't roll a "3" when you throw one die.

You can compute:

P(Not 3) = $\frac{\text{Total number of numbers that aren't 3 on die}}{\text{Total number of numbers on die}}$ = $\frac{5}{6}$

However, you can compute this by following the probability rule that
P(Not 3) = 1 − P(3)

Therefore, P(Not 3) = 1 − $\frac{1}{6}$ = $\frac{5}{6}$

Conditional Probability

What is Conditional Probability? Conditional probability looks at the probability that more than one event occurs. Conditional probability deals with dependent events and is also referred to as compound probability.

Conditional Probability is denoted as P(B|A) which says the "Probability of event B given that event A has occurred." The equation for Conditional Probability is:

P(A∩B) = P(B|A)P(A)

What are Dependent Events? Two events are dependent if the outcome of one event depends on the outcome of the other event.

What are Mutually Exclusive Events? Mutually exclusive events are two events that can NOT happen at the same time.

Example of Dependent (or Compound) Probability:
You have a bag filled with 6 marbles. 2 marbles are White, 2 marbles are Green, and 2 marbles are Yellow. Note: The marbles will not be replaced or placed back in the bag.

What is the probability that you will first pick a Green marble and then pick a White marble without looking?

Total Number of Outcomes = 6 marbles

First Pick (6 marbles):

$$P(\text{White}) = \frac{2}{6}$$

$$P(\text{Green}) = \frac{2}{6}$$

$$P(\text{Yellow}) = \frac{2}{6}$$

Second Pick: (5 marbles left in the bag)

$$P(\text{White}) = \frac{2}{5}$$

$$P(\text{Green}) = \frac{1}{5}$$

$$P(\text{Yellow}) = \frac{2}{5}$$

Therefore, P(Green ∩ White) = P(White|Green)P(Green)

$P(\text{Green}) = \frac{2}{6}$ $\qquad$ $P(\text{White|Green}) = \frac{2}{5}$

$P(\text{Green} \cap \text{White}) = \frac{2}{5} * \frac{2}{6} = \frac{4}{30} = \frac{2}{15}$

Simple Probability

What is randomness and probability? In statistics, randomness does not mean unpredictable or haphazard, but rather it refers to a phenomenon in which individual outcomes are uncertain, but which follow a predictable and calculable distribution after many repetitions. This predictable distribution, or long term relative frequency, is referred to as probability. Probability is always represented by a number between 0 and 1, or as a percentage. Therefore, the greatest value a probability can take is 1 (or 100%), and the lowest value is 0.

What is a sample space? A sample space is the set of all possible outcomes. For example, the sample space when rolling a standard die is S= {1, 2, 3, 4, 5, 6}. Each possible outcome is called an event.

What is the Multiplication Principle? The multiplication principle states that if two tasks are independent, and you can do task one x number of ways, and task two y number of ways, then the number of ways the two can be done together is x times y.

> **Example of the Multiplication Principle:** A girl has fourteen pairs of pants, sixteen shirts, and three pairs of shoes. How many possible outfit combinations does she have?
>
> According to the multiplication principle:
>
> (# shirts) × (# pants) × (# shoes) = total combinations
>
> (16) × (14) × (3) = total combinations = 672 different outfits

What is the Addition Rule? The addition rule states that if two events are disjoint, or in other words if two events cannot occur at the same time, then $P(A or B) = P(A) + P(B)$. This is also referred to as a union, and is written $P(A \cup B) = P(A) + P(B)$. This equation is only valid for disjoint events.

> **Example of the Addition Rule:** There is a .5 probability that a teacher will give an assignment greater than 10 problems on any given day. There is a .1 probability that the teacher will give a quiz on any given day. Assuming that the teacher will never give a homework assignment greater than 10 problems and a quiz on the same day, what is the probability of having either a quiz or a homework assignment larger than 10 problems?
>
> Because the events are disjoint, the addition rule applies.

P(more than 10 problems)=P(quiz)= P(quiz or a homework assignment larger than 10 problems)

.5+.1=.6

There is a .6 probability of having either a quiz or a homework assignment greater than 10 problems.

If two events are NOT disjoint, the equation $P(A \cup B) = P(A) + P(B) - P(A \cap B)$ is used. The event $P(A \cap B)$ is called an intersection, and is the probability that events A and B occur together (see the multiplication rule for further explanation).

What is the Complement Rule? A complement is the event that a specific event will not occur. In other words, the complement of a certain probability is probability that something does not happen. The complement of event A is expressed as A^c. The complement rule is expressed by the following equation:

$$P(A^c) = 1 - P(A)$$

Example of the Complement Rule: The probability that it will rain on any particular day in a given city is P(R)=.3. What then is the probability that it will not rain?

The probability that it will not rain is the complement of it raining, therefore the complement rule can be used.

$P(R^c) = 1 - P(R)$

$P(R^c) = 1 - .3$

$P(R^c) = .7$

What is the Multiplication Rule? There are two different multiplication rules. The first is used in the case of independent events. Two events are independent if the outcome of one event does NOT affect the outcome of the other. The equation is $P(A \cap B) = P(A)P(B)$, or in words "the probability of A intersect B is the probability of A multiplied by the probability of B." When two events are not independent, the equation is $P(A \cap B) = P(A)P(B|A)$, or in words "the probability of A intersect B is the probability of A multiplied by the probability of B given A."

Example of the Multiplication Rule: The probability that a given student will forget their homework on any given day is P(H)=.1. The probability that the same student will forget a writing implement on any given day is P(W)= .6. Assuming the two events to be independent, what is the probability of a student forgetting both their homework, and a writing implement?

$P(H \cap W) = P(H)P(W)$

$P(H \cap W) = (.1)(.6)$

$P(H \cap W) = .06$

The probability that a student will forget both homework and writing implement is .06.

What do independent and disjoint mean? Independent means that one outcome does not affect the probability of another outcome. Disjoint means that two outcomes can never occur together. It is not possible for something to be both disjoint and independent, because if something is disjoint then the outcome of the first event will affect the possibilities of the second.

Z Scores

What are z scores? Z scores are also called standard units. This is because z scores are used to analyze data, not in terms of numerical value, but in terms of distance from the mean. The units of z scores are standard deviations. This means that a z score of 1 would describe a value which is 1 standard deviation, or σ, away from the mean μ. Z scores are generally used in determining percentiles and probabilities. Z scores can only be used when data follows a Normal distribution.

What is the formula for z scores? Z scores are calculated using the formula $z = \frac{x - \mu}{\sigma}$.

What is a density curve/Normal distribution? The best way to picture a density curve is to imagine the histogram for a set of data. If you try to draw a single fluid line to show the shape of the histogram, you will have come up with the density curve for the data. The density curve is always shown on a horizontal axis, and the area underneath it is always equal to exactly one. The relative position of a piece of data in a density curve is used in determining probability and percentiles. The most useful and well known density curves are called Normal density curves. These follow the stereotypical bell shape. In a Normal curve the mean and median are exactly equal. A Normal curve is pictured below.

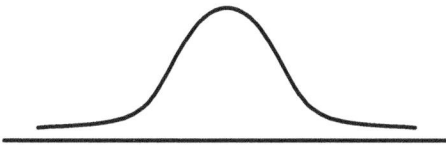

How are z-scores used? Z scores are used to determine percentiles and probabilities by using the properties of a Normal density curve. Because z scores are a standard measurement, there is a ratio of where a z score is, and what part of the curve it describes. Because density curves have a total area of 1 under the curve, the position of a z score correlates to a specific percentile. For example, a z score of 1.55 in a Normal distribution receives the values .9394, which means that it is at or above 93.94% of the data. In other words it is the 93rd percentile. A table with some of these probabilities can be found at the back of the book.

Example 1: The ages of a certain population follow a Normal distribution in which $\mu = 45$ and $\sigma = 15$. How many standard deviations, or standard units, away from the population mean is a person who is 35 years old?

Standard units are calculated as z scores. Therefore, since $z = \dfrac{x - \mu}{\sigma}$, using the information given in the problem:

$$z = \dfrac{35 - 45}{15} = -.67$$

A 35 year old person is .67 standard deviations *below* the mean. Notice that instead of giving a negative value, the word below is used to indicate the position of the answer.

Example 2: What is the standard deviation of a set of data in which a data point of value 12 falls in a distribution such that $z = -1.2$, when $\mu = 20$?

Because we know μ, x, and z, the standard deviation can be reverse calculated using the formula for a *z* score. First substitute the values that are known, and then solve for σ.

$$z = \dfrac{x - \mu}{\sigma}$$

$$-1.2 = \frac{12-20}{\sigma}$$

and $\sigma = 6.67$.

Example 3: The heights of a certain population in inches follows a Normal distribution such that $\mu = 67$ and $\sigma = 10$. What percentage of the population is between 60 and 70 inches tall?

This can be determined using z scores. First, determine the z scores for the two values.

$$z_{60} = \frac{x - \mu}{\sigma} = \frac{60 - 67}{10} = -.7$$

$$z_{70} = \frac{x - \mu}{\sigma} = \frac{70 - 67}{10} = .3$$

Then, determine the percentiles of the two z scores.

$z = -.7$ is .2420

$z = .3$ is .6179

Because we want to know the percentage of the data that falls between the two points we subtract the two values.

.6179 − .2420 = .3759.

Therefore, 37.59% of the population has a height between 60 and 70 inches.

Empirical Rule

What is the Empirical Rule? The Empirical Rule is a way of analyzing a Normal distribution in terms of standard deviation. It is also called the 65-95-99.5 Rule because it states that approximately 65% of the observations will fall within one standard deviation σ of the mean μ of a Normal distribution, 95% of the observations will fall within two standard deviations 2σ of the mean μ of a Normal distribution, and 99.5% of the observations will fall within three standard deviations 3σ of the mean μ of a Normal distribution.

Example: A data set follows a Normal distribution, and has $\mu = 50$ and $\sigma = 5$. What percent of the data is between the values $x = 45$ and $x = 55$?

The Empirical rule states that 65% of the observations will fall within σ of the mean of a Normal distribution.

$\mu - \sigma = 50 - 5 = 45$
$\mu + \sigma = 50 + 5 = 55$

Therefore 45 and 55 are the two values within σ of the mean, and 65% of the observations will lie within the range.

Example: A data sets follows a Normal distribution, where $\mu = 75$ and $\sigma = 15$. What values will the top 2.5% of the observations take?

The Empirical rule states that 95% of the data will fall within 2σ of the mean of a Normal distribution. That leaves 5% unaccounted for, 2.5% of which will fall above the range, and 2.5% of which will fall below the range. Therefore, the top 2.5% of the observations fall at or above the value $\mu + 2\sigma$.

$\mu + 2\sigma$
$= 75 + 2(15)$
$= 75 + 30$
$= 105$

The top 2.5% of observations fall within the range $x \geq 105$.

Example: Knowing that a data set follows a Normal distribution with $\mu = 60$, and where the bottom 2.5% of the data falls where $x \leq 20$, determine the standard deviation of the data set.

The Empirical rule states that 95% of the data will fall within 2σ of the mean of a Normal distribution. Therefore, since the lower 2.5% of the data falls at or below 20, and the lower 2.5% of the data falls 2σ below the mean, and that information can be used to reverse calculate σ.

$20 = \mu - 2\sigma$
$20 = 60 - 2\sigma$
$2\sigma = 40$
$\sigma = 20$

The standard deviation of the data set is 20.

Correlation and Regression

What is correlation? Correlation refers to the extent to which variables satisfy an equation or criteria in a situation. An example of perfect correlation would be the well known formula for area of a rectangle which is $A = LW$. The variables in this formula are perfectly correlated due to the nature of the equals sign and equation properties.

Another example of correlation would be to compare to situations or events. The height and weight of individuals has some correlation, but not a perfect correlation.

What does correlation mean? When two variables have a correlation, it means that there is an association between them. In a positive correlation, or positive association, as one variable increases, the other increases as well. In the case of a negative correlation, as one variable increases, the other decreases. It is important to remember that association does not imply causation. What this means is that just because a correlation exists, does not prove that one event causes the other. An example of this is that the amount of people who drown and ice cream consumption tend to have a positive correlation, however the reason is not that eating ice cream causes a person to drown, but because the instances of each increase during summer months.

What is regression? Regression is an estimation of one variable based on one or more related variables. The estimated variable is called the dependent variable. The dependent variable is estimated from the original independent variable(s).

What is linear correlation? Linear correlation occurs when all the points on a scatter diagram appear to lie close to a line.

What is the coefficient of determination? The coefficient of determination is basically a fancy description of r^2, the square of the correlation. When correlation is used to determine the linearity of a particular scatterplot, and a line of best fit is calculated, there will generally be values which do not fit the line exactly. Therefore, when using the line to predict the variable, the results will not always be exact. The coefficient of determination, or r^2, describes the extent to which that natural variation is explained by the least squares regression line.

How is correlation used to make an equation? If a scatterplot has a high correlation, it makes sense to create an equation of a line to describe it. This is done using residuals. The residual is the vertical distance from the line of best fit to the points which do not lie precisely on it. Because some values will lie above the line, and some below, the idea is to make the total sum as close to zero as possible. This is called the least squares regression line. The slope of the least squares regression line follows the formula $m = r \dfrac{s_y}{s_x}$, and the line will always go through the point ($\bar{x}$, $\bar{y}$) where x is the explanatory variable and y is the response variable. This information can be used to calculate the line. It is important however to remember that such lines are usually only accurate for the range the data falls within. The farther out of range, the more incorrect it becomes. Also, correlation and regression only apply to data with a linear relation.

> **Example**: Two data sets have a correlation of .87. The mean and standard deviation of the explanatory variable are 7 and 2 respectively, and the mean and standard deviation of the response variable are 10 and 6 respectively. What is the least squares regression line for the data?
>
> All of the information is known except the y intercept of the data, so use the slope intercept formula to determine it.
>
> Therefore $\hat{y} = 2.61x - 8.27$. Using the variable $\hat{y}$ signifies that the line is not an actual representation of the data, but rather a best estimate based on the data.
>
> **What is extrapolation?** Extrapolation is the term used when attempting to use a regression line to calculate values which are outside the range of the data. This is generally very unreliable.

Scatter Diagram

What is a scatter diagram? A scatter diagram displays the locations and relationships of two variables (X, Y) on a rectangular coordinate system.

Following is an example of a scatter diagram for the following data:

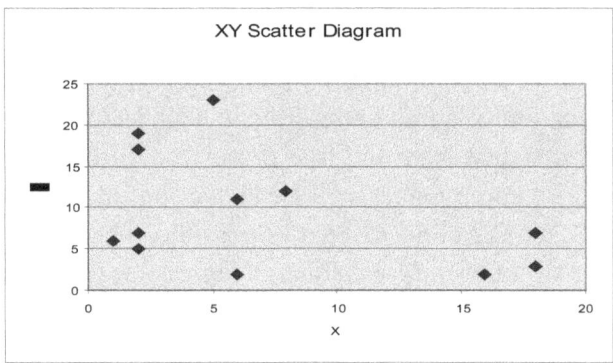

It is difficult to draw a line that is close to most of the points on the previous XY scatter diagram. In this case the data points are considered to have little or no correlation.

Positive Linear Correlation

The following is an example of a positive linear correlation: Y tends to increase as X increases.

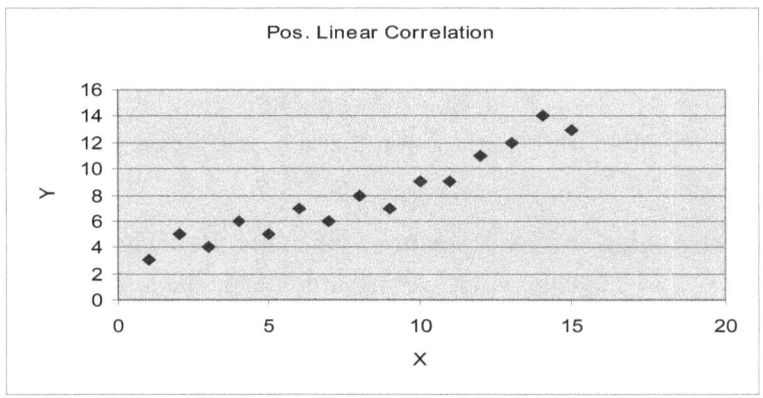

Negative Linear Correlation

The following is an example of negative linear correlation: Y tends to decrease as X increases.

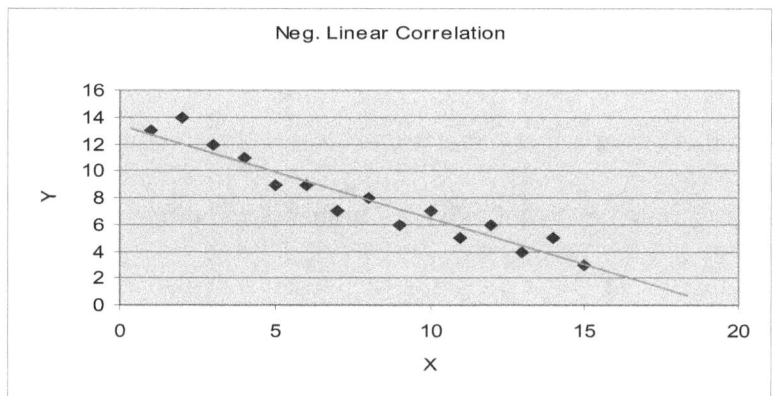

What does the red line in the scatter diagram represent? The red line in the scatter diagram represents the line of best fit which demonstrates the relationship between two variables x and y. The relationship is depicted by showing the amount one variable increases or decreases with regards to the other variable.

The line of best fit should represent an "average" of all the data points. Since it is an "average", many of the data points will not fall directly on the line of best fit. The line of best fit allows you to estimate values in place of finding the actual values.

How do you construct the line of best fit? You can manually find the line of best fit on a piece of graph paper. Plot the data points in an xy scatter diagram. Separate the data points into two groups by constructing a vertical line with half of the data points to the left of it and half the data points to the right of it.

Find the mid point on the both the x and y axis for both groups. Plot these two center points in the xy scatter diagram. Draw a line that connects the two center points. This is an estimation of the line of best fit.

Another method to find the line of best fit is to use linear regression.

 Correlation Coefficient

What is the correlation coefficient? The correlation coefficient depicts the degree of relationship between predicted values and actual values. The correlation coefficient is a number between 0 and 1 and is represented by the variable *r*.

If *r* = 0 then there is no correlation between the variables.

If *r* = 1 then there is a perfect correlation between the variables.

Therefore, it is more beneficial to have a higher correlation.

The correlation coefficient for a set of observations $(x_i, y_i) : i = 1,\ldots,n$ is:

$$r = \frac{1}{n-1} \sum \left(\frac{x_i - \bar{x}}{Sx}\right)\left(\frac{y_i - \bar{y}}{Sy}\right)$$

 Linear Regression

How do you find linear regression? The least-squares regression line of *Y* on *X* can be found using the equation.

$$y = \beta_0 + \beta_1 x$$

Where *y* = dependent variable
  x = independent variable
  β_0 = *y* − intercept
  β_1 = slope of the line

Permutations

What are permutations? A permutation is an ordered sequence of items taken from a set of distinct items <u>without replacement</u>.

To find the number of permutations of

$$_nP_r = \frac{n!}{(n-r)!}$$

Remember "!" means factorial where $n! = n(n-1)(n-2)\ldots(1)$
$3! = 3 * 2 * 1 = 6$
$6! = 6 * 5 * 4 * 3 * 2 * 1 = 720$

Example of a permutation: Find the number of permutations of the numbers 2, 4, 6 taken two at a time.

Therefore, n = number of distinct items = 3
r = number of numbers in each group = 2

$$_3P_2 = \frac{3!}{(3-2)!} = \frac{3!}{(1)!} = \frac{3*2*1}{1} = 6$$

You can also find the number of permutations by listing all the possibilities:

2, 4
2, 6
4, 2
4, 6
6, 2
6, 4

Note: In permutations that 2,6 and 6,2 are considered to be separate results.

Combinations

What are combinations? A combination is an unordered subset of items taken from a group of distinct items.

$$\binom{n}{k} = \frac{n!}{k!(n-k)!}$$

Example of a combination: Find the number of combinations for the numbers 2, 4, 6 taken two at a time.

Therefore, n = number of distinct items = 3
k = number of numbers in each group = 2

$$\binom{n}{k} = \frac{n!}{k!(n-k)!} = \binom{3}{2} = \frac{3!}{2!(3-2)!} = \frac{3!}{2!(1)!} = \frac{3*2*1}{2*1*1} = \frac{6}{2} = 3$$

There are only 3 combinations which include:
2,4
2,6
4,6

Remember in combinations 2,4 and 4,2 are considered the same result and are NOT counted twice.

Binomial Formula

What is the binomial formula? The binomial formula is represented by the binomial distribution. The binomial distribution corresponds to successive terms of the binomial formula.

Following is the binomial formula:

$$(q+p)^N = q^N + \binom{N}{1} q^{N-1} p + \binom{N}{2} q^{N-2} p^2 + ... + p^N$$

Where 1, $\binom{N}{1}$, and $\binom{N}{2}$ are binomial coefficients.

🎓 Discrete and Continuous Random Variables

What is a discrete random variable? A discrete random variable is any variable which has a specific and countable number of possible values. The probabilities for all the possible values of the variable must take a value between 0 and 1, and when summed together they must all add to precisely one.

Example: A deck of cards contains values between one and five. If the probability of drawing any specific number follows the following distribution, what is the probability of drawing a four?

Card Value:	1	2	3	4	5
Probability:	.4	.2	.1	?	.1

The sum of all the possibilities must add up to one. Therefore the probability of drawing a four is 1- P(1)-P(2)-P(3)-P(5) which equals 1-.4-.2-.1-.1 which equals .2.

What is a continuous random variable? A continuous random variable differs from a discrete random variable because it does not have a countable number of outcomes. For example, whole numbers between 1 and 5 would be a discrete random variable with sample space S={2, 3, 4}. However, the description, any number between 0 and 1 would be a continuous random variable because there are infinite amounts of numbers between 0 and 1, and therefore the sample space S={all numbers x such that $0 \leq x \leq 1$} is not countable. Probability of a continuous random variable cannot be calculated for individual occurrences, but must be calculated over a range. As with discrete random variables, the total sum of the probabilities must add to 1.

What is the mean of a discrete random variable? The mean of a discrete random variable is calculated with the equation $\mu_x = \sum x_i p_i$. In other words, the mean of a discrete random variable is the sum of each variable multiplied by its corresponding probability.

Example: A person is playing a game of chance with a weighted die for which the probabilities of rolling any number follow the following distribution. What is the mean amount which is rolled using this die?

Value on die:	1	2	3	4	5	6
Probability:	.1	.1	.3	.3	.1	.1

$$\mu_x = \sum x_i p_i$$
$$\mu_x = 1(.1) + 2(.1) + 3(.3) + 4(.3) + 5(.1) + 6(.1)$$
$$\mu_x = 3.5$$

The mean roll of the die is 3.5.

What is the variance of a discrete random variable? The variance of a discrete random variable is calculated using the equation $\sigma_x^2 = \sum(x_i - \mu_x)^2 p_i$. In other words, variance is the sum of the square of each value minus the mean multiplied by its probability. The reason the equation is expressed as σ_x^2 is because the standard deviation of a discrete random variable is determined by taking the square root of the variance.

Example: What is the standard deviation of the die described in the previous example?

Knowing that the mean is 3.5, variance is:

$$\sigma_x^2 = \sum(x_i - \mu_x)^2 p_i$$
$$\sigma_x^2 = (1-3.5)^2(.1) + (2-3.5)^2(.1) + (3-3.5)^2(.3) + (4-3.5)^2(.3) + (5-3.5)^2(.1) + (6-3.5)^2(.1)$$
$$\sigma_x^2 = .625 + .225 + .075 + .075 + .225 + .625$$
$$\sigma_x^2 = 1.85$$

Knowing that standard deviation is the square root of variance:

$$\sigma_x = \sqrt{\sigma_x^2} = \sqrt{1.85} = 1.36$$

What is the Law of Large Numbers? The Law of Large Numbers states that the more observations that are made, or the large the sample size is, the closer the probability of the sample comes to the probability of the population. For example, the more times a coin in flipped, the closer the ratio between heads and tails comes to being exactly .5.

What are the calculations for a continuous random variable? Continuous random variables are generally only calculated when their distributions follow two different forms. One is in the case of a uniform distribution. When a continuous random variable is uniform, then all of the values have the same probability. Picture it like a box on a coordinate plot. Because the total area of the box must equal one, then the box must have the dimensions one by one. Therefore, the "area under the curve" between any two points is just the difference between them. The other case is when the variable follows a Normal distribution. In this case z scores can be used to determine probability because the area under a Normal curve must also equal exactly one.

Example: If a variable follows a uniform distribution, what is the probability of the result lying between the values of .5 and .8?

Because the distribution is uniform, each value has an equal chance of being chosen, and therefore the probability is calculated as the difference between the two or, .8-5=.3.

 Chance Models and Sampling

What is sampling in statistics? Sampling theory is the study of relationships between a population and samples taken from the population. Sampling theory allows you to determine whether observed differences between two samples are a result of chance or whether they are statistically significant. It is critical to have samples that are accurate representations of the population.

How can you find a representative sample of a population? One method is to engage in random sampling. Random sampling occurs when each member of a population has an equal chance of being included in the sample. This can be achieved by drawing numbers at random or using a list of random numbers.

Samples can be taken from a population with or without replacement. Populations can be finite or infinite in nature. An example of a finite population would be to choose 4 cards from a deck of 52 cards. The finite population is the 52 cards. An example of an infinite population would be to roll a pair of dice ten times and count the number of times a 7 is rolled.

What is expected value? Expectation helps you to determine whether or not a statistic is biased. A statistics is unbiased if its expectation equals the corresponding population parameter.

$\bar{X}$ and $\hat{s}^2$ are examples of unbiased estimates because $E\{\bar{X}\} = \mu$ and $E\{\hat{s}^2\} = \sigma^2$.

Note: σ^2 is the population variance.

Sampling Distributions

What is the difference between a parameter and a statistic? A parameter is a value or probability which describes a population as a whole. Generally in true situations the parameters is not known because it is impractical or impossible to study an entire population. A parameter is signified by p. A statistic is a value or probability which is computed through the study of a sample. Statistics are often used in real life situations to estimate or describe a parameter. A statistic is signified by $\hat{p}$.

The mean of a sample: In order to differentiate between the mean of a parameter versus the mean of a statistic, the two are represented by different variables. The mean of a parameter is μ, and the mean of a statistic is $\bar{x}$.

What is sampling variability? Because it isn't practical to determine parameters, samples are used. However, using a single sample leaves a lot of room for bias. This is called sampling variability. In other words, individual samples are likely to vary greatly from one to the next.

What is a sampling distribution? Because of sampling variability, sampling distributions are used to get as close as possible to the true parameter. The sampling distribution is the distribution of values of all possible samples of the same size from the same population. The more samples are taken, the closer a sample comes to a Normal distribution, and also the closer the mean of the statistic comes to describing the parameter.

Mean and standard deviation of a sampling distribution: The mean of a sampling distribution $\mu_{\hat{p}}$ is exactly the parameter. In other words, $\hat{p} = p$. This is because a perfect sampling distribution will take the form of a Normal curve centered about the parameter. Normalcy should only be assumed when the sample size is large enough such that np≥10 and n(1-p)≥1. The standard deviation of a sampling distribution $\sigma_{\hat{p}} = \sqrt{\dfrac{p(1-p)}{n}}$. This equation should only be used when the population size N is at least ten times as large as the sample size n. In other words, when N≥10n.

Mean and standard deviation of a sample mean: When a large number of samples are used, the distribution of their means should be such that the mean of the sample $\mu_{\bar{x}} = \mu$, and the standard deviation of the means $\sigma_{\bar{x}} = \frac{\sigma}{\sqrt{n}}$.

Central Limit Theorem: The Central Limit Theorem states that a sample of size n from a population with mean µ and finite standard deviation σ for which n is large will approximately follow a normal distribution $N(\mu, \frac{\sigma}{\sqrt{n}})$. In other words, if a sample is large, the sampling distribution will have a Normal distribution.

Example: A lawyer in a large firm wishes to know the average number of cases won by the lawyers in his firm. He conducts a random survey of 300 of the 3000 lawyers. In the survey he asks how many cases each of the lawyers has won. His sample yields a mean of 37 cases, and he knows that the standard deviation of the whole firm is 12 cases. What can be concluded?

Because the sample is so large the Central Limit Theorem states that the mean of the whole firm will be 37 as well, and the standard deviation of his data will be $\frac{\sigma}{\sqrt{n}} = \frac{12}{\sqrt{300}} = .69$

 Confidence Intervals

How do you measure the accuracy of your sample estimates? Sample estimate accuracy can be measured using confidence interval estimates of population parameters. Intervals provide more accuracy then a single number or pinpoint estimate.

What are confidence intervals? Confidence intervals are based on a normal distribution with a mean of μ_s and a standard deviation of σ_s for a sample statistic S.

Since it is a normal distribution we expect to find a sample statistic S lying in the following intervals and corresponding percentages:

Interval	Percentage
$\mu_s - \sigma_s$ to $\mu_s + \sigma_s$	68.27%
$\mu_s - 2\sigma_s$ to $\mu_s + 2\sigma_s$	95.45%
$\mu_s - 3\sigma_s$ to $\mu_s + 3\sigma_s$	99.73%

We can apply this methodology to the sample statistic S. This means we would expect to find μ_s in the intervals listed in the following table the corresponding percentage of the time.

Interval	Percentage
$S \pm \sigma_s$	68.27%
$S \pm 2\sigma_s$	95.45%
$S \pm 3\sigma_s$	99.73%

What is the confidence level? The confidence level refers to the percentage confidence.

How are Confidence Intervals Calculated? A confidence interval is calculated using the formula $\bar{x} \pm z^* \dfrac{\sigma}{\sqrt{n}}$ where $\bar{x}$ is the mean of the sample, and σ is the standard deviation of the population.

What are critical values? Critical values are denoted with the variable z*. Critical values are used in calculating confidence intervals, and they represent the z score for which a certain amount of data is represented.

Example of finding a critical value: What critical value would be used to calculate a 70% confidence interval? To figure out the 70% confidence interval the location of the middle 70%, or in terms of the normal curve the middle .7, of data are. 1-.7 is .3, and that is divided between the two ends so it's .15. This means that the z score used is the once which excludes the .15, which is approximately z=.104.

Example of a confidence interval: If a population has $\sigma = 25$, and a 100 person sample yields a sample mean of 185, construct a 95% confidence interval.

For a 95% confidence interval z* is 1.960. Therefore, the confidence interval is

$$\bar{x} \pm z^* \dfrac{\sigma}{\sqrt{n}}$$

$$185 \pm 1.960 \left(\dfrac{25}{\sqrt{100}} \right)$$

Plug in the known values.

And the confidence interval is (180.9, 189.9)

Note: It is important to recognize that a confidence interval does NOT describe the *probability* that a number will be in a certain interval, but rather the confidence with which we say that it is in the interval.

Margin of error: Margin of error is a calculation of how precise the values determined by a sampling distribution are to the actual parameter. This is determined with the following formula where z* is the critical value of a standard Normal distribution.

$$\text{Margin of error } m = z^* \frac{\sigma}{\sqrt{n}}$$

What are t scores? The above calculations make the unrealistic assumption that the population standard deviation is known. In practice this will rarely be the case, and therefore only the standard deviation of the sample is known. T scores are used in place of z scores when this is the case. If t scores are used the formula for a confidence interval changes to be $\bar{x} \pm t^* \frac{s}{\sqrt{n}}$. Like the values for z scores, the corresponding t* can be found using a table which pairs sample size to "upper tail probability." This table can be found at the back of the book. For sample size, use the number that is one less than the actual size of the sample.

Example of t score calculations: Using the following sample, construct an 80% confidence interval for the mean.

15	16	18	12	17
9	5	3	4	18
15	25	39	16	18
14	38	15	14	17

Using the information given we can determine that $\bar{x} = 16.4$, $s_x = 9.2$, and $n = 20$. To construct an 80% confidence interval t*=1.328. Therefore, by substituting this information into the equation

$$\bar{x} \pm t^* \frac{s}{\sqrt{n}}$$

$$16.4 \pm 1.328 \left(\frac{9.2}{\sqrt{20}} \right)$$

we are able to determine that the confidence interval is (13.49, 19.31)

Standard error: Standard error is basically the standard deviation of a statistic, or how far off it is expected that the statistic may be. This is used in place of the formula $\sigma/\sqrt{n}$ when the standard deviation of the population is not known, and the statistic must be used instead. The standard error of a sample mean is calculated with the following formula:

$$\text{Standard Error} = \frac{s}{\sqrt{n}}$$

Tests of Significance

How do you test statistical significance? Statistical significance can help you make decisions. First, you need to create a null hypothesis.

What is a null hypothesis? A null hypothesis refers to a statement you wish to test. For example, your null hypothesis may be that you will find no difference between the test scores of girls versus boys at a specific school. Here null hypothesis is denoted by Y_0.

Y_0 = There is **no** difference between the tests scores of girls versus boys at a specific school.

You can also create an alternative hypothesis. An alternative hypothesis is denoted by Y_0.

Y_0 = Girls will yield higher test scores than boys at this specific school.

The purpose of a hypothesis is to accept or reject it. To do this the following formula is used:

$$z = \frac{\text{estimate} - \text{hypothesized value}}{\text{standard deviation of estimate}} \quad \text{OR} \quad \frac{x - \mu_0}{\sigma/n}$$

If the z score is realistic, it may be accepted.

How do you accept or reject a hypothesis? You can use tests of significance to accept or reject a hypothesis. Testing a hypothesis also involves dealing with Type I and Type II errors.

A Type I error occurs when you reject a hypothesis that should have been accepted. A Type II error occurs when you accept a hypothesis when it should have been rejected.

Tests of significance present the maximum probability with which you would be willing to risk a Type I error. The significance level is denoted by α. You will specify the significance level α. Values for α are usually 0.05 or 0.01.

A $\alpha = 0.05$ means there is a 5% chance that you would commit a Type I error (reject the hypothesis when it should have been accepted.) This in turn means that you can be 95% confident that you have made the correct decision regarding the hypothesis.

A $\alpha = 0.01$ means there is a 1% chance that you would commit a Type I error. This in turn means that you can be 99% confident that you have made the correct decision regarding the hypothesis.

The above is an example of tests involving normal distributions.

This normal distribution represents a 95% confidence level. (Each critical region represents 1/2 of 0.05).

This means that we can be 95% confident that if the hypothesis is true then the z score of an actual sample statistic, S will lie between -1.96 and 1.96. If the z statistics lies out of this range then we can reject the hypothesis.

What are P Values? The null hypothesis Y_o is the statement we want to prove or disprove, this is done using the alternative hypothesis Y_a. By gathering data that shows Y_o is true it makes it unlikely that Y_o is true. This is done using P values. If a p value is high, there is no evidence against Y_o. If a p value is low that means there is strong evidence against Y_o.

> **Example:** The mayor of a city wishes to know the average response time of ambulances after a 911 call. The year before the average response time was $\mu = 6.7$ with $\sigma = 2$. The next year he takes a random sample of 400 response times to determine if their time has improved, and finds that they are $\bar{x} = 6.48$. Therefore, in this case, $Y_o : \mu = 6.7$ minutes and $Y_a : \mu < 6.7$ minutes.
>
> The equation for the z score is $z = \dfrac{\bar{x} - \mu_o}{\dfrac{\sigma}{\sqrt{n}}}$

By using the information we can determine that $z = \dfrac{6.48 - 6.7}{\frac{2}{\sqrt{400}}} = \dfrac{-.22}{.1} = -2.2$

This is more than two standard deviations away from the mean, which makes it very probable that Y_a is correct because it is unlikely that a random sample would have a score so far away from the true mean.

What is the x^2 test? This is called the "Chi-square" test using the chi-square distribution.

The x^2 statistic is defined as follows:

$$x^2 = \frac{Ns^2}{\sigma^2} = \frac{(X_1 - \bar{X})^2 + (X_2 - \bar{X})^2 + \ldots + (X_N - \bar{X})^2}{\sigma^2}$$

Where N is the sample size, σ is the standard deviation, and $\bar{X}$ is the sample mean.

The chi-square distribution written in standard form is as follows:

$$Y = Y_0 x^{\sigma - 2} e^{-(1/2) x^2}$$

Where Y_0 is a constant depending on σ such that the total area under the curve is 1. $\sigma = N - 1$ and is known as the number of degrees of freedom.

You test the hypothesis in a similar manner to the z test except you use the x^2 statistic reference table instead.

Comparing Sample Means

What are two sample problems? One main use of statistics is comparison. For example, to determine which medicine works better, which gum flavor lasts longer, or which shoe works better, statistics must be used. Situations involving comparing two populations or means or treatments are called two sample problems. The main question in these cases is whether or not the difference in the results is statistically significant, which can be a subjective claim.

How are two samples compared? When both samples have a roughly Normal distribution, a comparison of the means is most useful. For two samples to be compared they must meet three conditions: They must have been two SRS's from two distinct X populations, they must be approximately Normal in distribution, and the samples must be independent. When this is the case then the distribution of the statistic $\bar{x}_1 - \bar{x}_2$ is Normal as well.

How are z statistics calculated in two sample problems? Because the distribution $\bar{x}_1 - \bar{x}_2$ is Normally distributed, many of the same basic equations can be used in two sample problems as in single sample problems. For example, instead of $\bar{x} = \mu_x$ as is the case in one sample problems, in two sample problems $\bar{x}_1 - \bar{x}_2 = \mu_1 - \mu_2$. The variance of a two sample problem is $\dfrac{\sigma_1^2}{n_1} + \dfrac{\sigma_2^2}{n_2}$. Knowing this, the equation for the z statistic can be determined.

$$z = \frac{(\bar{x}_1 - \bar{x}_2) - (\mu_1 - \mu_2)}{\sqrt{\dfrac{\sigma_1^2}{n_1} + \dfrac{\sigma_2^2}{n_2}}}$$

As you can see, the equation is essentially just an elongated form of the regular z statistic formula.

Example: Use the following information to calculate the z statistic for the two data sets.

	Parameters			Statistics		
	Population Size	Mean	Standard Deviation	Sample Size	Mean	Standard deviation
Set 1:	100	65	12	10	68.7	10.2
Set 2:	150	76	5	15	73.2	7.8

$$z = \frac{(\bar{x}_1 - \bar{x}_2) - (\mu_1 - \mu_2)}{\sqrt{\dfrac{\sigma_1^2}{n_1} + \dfrac{\sigma_2^2}{n_2}}} = \frac{(68.7 - 73.2) - (65 - 76)}{\sqrt{\dfrac{12^2}{100} + \dfrac{5^2}{15}}} = \frac{(-4.5) - (-11)}{\sqrt{1.44 + 1.67}} = \frac{6.5}{3.11} = 2.09$$

Therefore, z=2.09

How are t statistics calculated in two sample problems? Just as it is unlikely that the standard deviation will be known in a one sample problem, it is unlikely that both standard deviations will be known in a two sample problem and therefore the t score is generally more useful than the z score. In a two sample problem the Standard Error formula is $SE = \sqrt{\dfrac{s_1^2}{n_1} + \dfrac{s_2^2}{n_2}}$. This can be used to determine the t statistic formula.

$$t = \frac{(\bar{x}_1 - \bar{x}_2) - (\mu_1 - \mu_2)}{\sqrt{\dfrac{s_1^2}{n_1} + \dfrac{s_2^2}{n_2}}}$$

As you can see, this equation is essentially the same as the regular t statistic formula, with some modifications.

STANDARD NORMAL PROBABILITIES

z	.00	.01	.02	.03	.04	.05	.06	.07	.08	.09
-3.4	.0003	.0003	.0003	.0003	.0003	.0003	.0003	.0003	.0003	.0002
-3.3	.0005	.0005	.0005	.0004	.0004	.0004	.0004	.0004	.0004	.0003
-3.2	.0007	.0007	.0006	.0006	.0006	.0006	.0006	.0005	.0005	.0005
-3.1	.0010	.0009	.0009	.0009	.0008	.0008	.0008	.0008	.0007	.0007
-3.0	.0013	.0013	.0013	.0012	.0012	.0011	.0011	.0011	.0010	.0010
-2.9	.0019	.0018	.0018	.0017	.0016	.0016	.0015	.0015	.0014	.0014
-2.8	.0026	.0025	.0024	.0023	.0023	.0022	.0021	.0021	.0020	.0019
-2.7	.0035	.0034	.0033	.0032	.0031	.0030	.0029	.0028	.0027	.0006
-2.6	.0047	.0045	.0044	.0043	.0041	.0040	.0039	.0038	.0037	.0036
-2.5	.0062	.0060	.0059	.0057	.0055	.0054	.0052	.0051	.0049	.0048
-2.4	.0082	.0080	.0078	.0075	.0073	.0071	.0069	.0068	.0066	.0064
-2.3	.0107	.0104	.0102	.0099	.0059	.0094	.0091	.0089	.0087	.0084
-2.2	.0139	.0136	.0132	.0129	.0125	.0122	.0119	.0116	.0113	.0110
-2.1	.0179	.0174	.0170	.0166	.0162	.0158	.0154	.0150	.0146	.0143
-2.0	.0228	.0222	.0217	.0212	.0207	.0202	.0197	.0192	.0188	.0183
-1.9	.0287	.0281	.0274	.0268	.0262	.0256	.0250	.0244	.0239	.0233
-1.8	.0359	.0351	.0344	.0336	.0329	.0322	.0314	.0307	.0301	.0294
-1.7	.0446	.0436	.0427	.0418	.0409	.0401	.0392	.0384	.0375	.0367
-1.6	.0548	.0537	.0526	.0516	.0505	.0595	.0485	.045	.0465	.0455
-1.5	.0668	.655	.0643	.060	.0618	.0606	.0594	.0582	.0571	.0559
-1.4	.0808	.0793	.0778	.0764	.0749	.0735	.0721	.0708	.0694	.0681
-1.3	.0968.	.0951	.0934	.0918	.0901	.0885	.0869	.0853	.0838	.0823
-1.2	.1151	1131	.1112	.1093	.1075	.1056	.108	.1020	.1003	.0985
-1.1	.1357	.1335	.1314	.1292	.1271	.1251	.1230	.1210	.1191	.1171
-1.0	.1587	1562	.1539	.1515	.1492	.1469	.1446	.1423	.1401	.1379
-.09	.1841	.1814	.1788	.1762	.1736	.1711	.1685	.1660	.1635	.1611
-0.8	.2119	.2090	.2061	.2033	.2005	.1977	.1949	.1922	.1894	.1867
-0.7	.2420	.2389	.2358	.2327	.2296	.2266	.2236	.2206	.2177	.2148
-0.6	.2743	.2709	.2676	.2643	.2611	.2578	.2546	.2514	.2483	.2451
-0.5	.3085	.3050	.3015	.2981	.2946	.2912	.2877	.2843	.2810	.2776
-0.4	.3446	.3409	.3372	.3336	.3300	.3264	.3228	.3192	.3156	.3121
-0.3	.3821	.3783	.3745	.3707	.3669	.3632	.3594	.3557	.3520	.3483
-0.2	.4207	.4168	.4129	.4090	.4052	.4013	.3974	.3936	.3897	.3859
-0.1	.4602	.4562	.4522	.4483	.4443	.4404	.4364	.4325	.4286	.4247
-0.0	.5000	.4960	.4920	.1880	.4840	.4801	.4761	.4721	.4681	.4641

STANDARD NORMAL PROBABILITIES (CONTINUED)

z	.00	.01	.02	.03	.04	.05	.06	.07	.08	.09
0.0	.5000	.5040	.5080	.5120	.5160	.5199	.5239	.5279	.5319	.5359
0.1	.5398	.5438	.5478	.5519	.5557	.5596	.5636	.5675	.5714	.5753
0.2	.5793	.5832	.5871	.5910	.5948	.5987	.6026	.6064	.6103	.6141
0.3	.6179	.6217	.6255	.6293	.6331	.6368	.6406	.6443	.6480	.6517
0.4	.6254	.6591	.6628	.6664	.6700	.6736	.6772	6808	.6844	.6879
0.5	.6915	.6950	.6985	.7019	.7054	.7088	.7123	.7157	.7190	.7224
0.6	.7257	.7291	.7324	.7357	7389	.7422	.7454	.7486	.7517	.7549
0.7	.7580	.7611	.7642	.7673	.7704	7734	.7764	.7794	7823	.7852
0.8	.7881	.7910	.7939	.7967	.7995	.8023	.8051	.8079	.8106	.8133
0.9	.8159	.8186	.8212	.8238	.8264	.8289	.8315	.8340	.8365	.8389
1.0	.8413	.8438	.8461	.8485	.8508	.8531	.8554	.8577	.8599	.8621
1.1	.8643	.8665	.8686	.8708	.8729	.8749	.8770	.8790	.8810	.8830
1.2	8849	.8849	.8888	.8907	.8925	.8944	.8962	.8980	.8997	.9015
1.3	.9032	.9049	.9066	.9082	.9099	.9115	.9131	.9147	.9162	.9177
1.4	.9192	.9207	.9222	.9236	.9251	.9265	.9279	.9292	.9306	.9319
1.5	.9332	.9345	.9357	.9370	.9382	.9394	.9406	.9418	.9429	.9441
1.6	.9452	.9463	.9474	.9484	.9495	.9505	.9515	.9525	.9535	.9545
1.7	.9554	.9564	.9573	.9582	.9591	.9599	.9608	.9616	.9625	.9633
1.8	.9641	.9649	.9656	.9664	.9671	.9678	.9686	.9693	.9699	.9706
1.9	.9713	.9719	.9726	.9732	.9738	.9744	.9750	.9756	.9761	.9767
2.0	.9772	.9778	.9783	.9788	.9793	.9798	.9803	.9808	.9812	.9817
2.1	.9821	.9826	.9830	.9834	.9838	.9842	.9846	.9850	.9854	.9857
2.2	.9861	.9864	.9868	.9871	.9875	.9878	.9881	.9884	.9887	.9890
2.3	.9893	.9896	.9898	.9901	.9904	.9906	.9909	.9911	.9913	.9916
2.4	.9918	.9920	.9922	.9925	.9927	.9929	.9931	.9932	.9934	.9936
2.5	.9938	.9940	.9941	.9943	.9945	.9946	.9948	.9949	.9951	.9952
2.6	.9953	.9955	.9956	.9957	.9959	.9960	.9961	.9962	.9963	.9964
2.7	.9965	.9966	.9967	.9968	.9969	.9970	.9971	.9972	.9973	.9974
2.8	.9974	.9975	.9976	.9977	.9977	.9978	.9979	.9979	.9980	.9981
2.9	.9981	.9982	.9982	.9983	.9984	.9984	.9985	.9985	.9986	.9986
3.0	.9987	.9987	.9987	.9988	.9988	.9989	.9989	.9989	.9990	.9990
3.1	.9990	.9991	.9991	.9991	.9992	.9992	.9992	.9992	.9993	.9993
3.2	.9993	.9993	.9994	.9994	.9994	.9994	.9994	.9995	.9995	.9995
3.3	.9995	.9995	.9995	.9996	.9996	.9996	.9996	.9996	.9996	.9997
3.4	.9997	.9997	.9997	.9997	.9997	.9997	.9997	.9997	.9997	.9998

T DISTRIBUTION CRITICAL VALUES

Upper Tail Probability

n	.25	.20	.15	.10	.05	.025	.02	.01	.005	.0025	.001	.0005
1	1.000	1.376	1.963	3.078	6.314	12.71	15.89	31.82	63.66	127.3	318.3	636.6
2	.816	1.061	1.386	1.886	2.920	4.303	4.849	6.965	9.925	14.09	22.33	31.60
3	0.765	0.978	1.250	1.638	2.353	3182	3.482	4.541	5.841	7.453	10.21	12.92
4	0.741	0.941	1.190	1.533	2.132	2.776	2.999	3.949	4.604	5.598	7.173	8.610
5	0.727	0.920	1.156	1.476	2.015	2.571	2.757	3.365	4.032	4.773	5.893	6.869
6	0.718	0.906	1.134	1.440	1.943	2.447	2.612	3.143	3.707	4.317	5.208	5.959
7	0.711	0.896	1.119	1.415	1.895	2.365	2.517	2.998	3.499	4.029	4.785	5.408
8	0.706	0.889	1.108	1.397	1.860	2.306	2.449	2.896	3.355	4833	4.501	5.041
9	0.703	0.883	1.100	1.383	1.833	2.262	2.389	2.821	3.250	3.690	4.297	4.781
10	0.700	0.879	1.093	1.372	1.812	2.228	2.359	2.764	3.169	3.581	4.144	4.587
11	0.697	0.876	1.088	1.363	1.796	2.201	2.328	2.718	3.106	3.497	4.025	4.437
12	0.695	0.873	1.083	1.356	1.782	2.179	2.303	2.681	3.055	3.428	3.930	4.318
13	0.694	0.870	1.079	1.350	1.771	2.160	2.282	2.650	3.012	3.372	3.852	4.221
14	0.692	0.868	1.076	1.345	1.761	2.145	2.264	2.624	3.977	3.326	3.787	4.140
15	0.691	0.866	1.074	1.341	1.753	2.131	2.249	2.602	2.947	3.286	3.733	4.076
16	0.690	0.865	1.071	1.337	1.746	2.120	2.235	2.583	2.921	3.252	3.686	4.015
17	0.689	0.863	1.069	1.333	1.740	2.110	2.224	2.567	2.898	3.222	3.646	3.965
18	0.688	0.862	1.067	1.330	1.734	2.101	2.214	2.552	2.878	3.197	3.611	3.922
19	0.688	0.861	1.066	1.328	1.729	2.093	2.205	2.539	2.861	3.174	3.579	3.883
20	0.687	0.860	1.064	1.325	1.725	2.086	2.197	2.528	2.845	3.153	3.552	3.850
21	0.686	0.859	1.063	1.323	1.721	2.080	2.189	2.518	2.831	3.135	3.527	3.819
22	0.685	0.858	1.061	1.321	1.717	2.074	2.183	2.509	2.819	3.119	3.505	3.792
23	0.685	0.858	1.060	1.319	1.714	2.069	2.177	2.500	2.807	3.104	3.485	3.768
24	0.684	0.857	1.059	1.318	1.711	2.064	2.172	2.492	2.797	3.091	3.467	3.745
25	0.684	0.856	1.058	1.316	1.708	2.060	2.167	2.485	2.787	3.078	3.450	3.725
26	0.684	0.856	1.058	1.315	1.706	2.056	2.162	2.479	2.779	3.067	3.435	3.707
27	0.683	0.855	1.057	1.314	1.703	2.052	2.158	2.473	2.771	3.057	3.421	3.690
28	0.683	0.855	1.056	1.313	1.701	2.048	2.154	2.467	2.763	3.047	3.408	3.674
29	0.683	0.854	1.055	1.311	1.699	2.045	2.150	2.462	2.756	3.038	3.396	3.659
30	0.681	0.854	1.055	1.310	1.697	2.042	2.147	2.457	2.750	3.030	3.285	3.646
40	0.679	0.851	1.050	1.303	1.684	2.021	2.123	2.423	2.704	2.971	3.207	3.551
50	0.679	0.849	1.047	1.299	1.76	2.009	2.109	2.403	2.678	2.937	3.261	3.496
60	0.678	0.848	1.045	1.296	1.671	1.000	2.099	2.390	2.660	2.915	3.232	3.460
80	0.677	0.846	1.043	1.292	1.664	1.990	2.088	2.374	2.639	2.887	3.195	3.416
100	0.675	0.845	1.042	1.290	1.660	1.984	2.081	2.364	2.626	2.871	3.174	3.390
1000	0.674	0.842	1.037	1.282	1.646	1.962	2.056	2.330	2.581	2.813	3.098	3.300
	50%	60%	70%0	80%	90%	95%	96%	98%	99%	99.5%	99.8%	99.9%

Confidence Level

Sample Questions

Foundation of Statistics (20)

For problems 1-2 use the following situation.

A campaign manager wishes to know how high approval is for his candidate. He decides to do a random survey of people with in the voting district. There are 10,000 people in the area, and he randomly selects 100 of them to poll.

1) What is the population size?

    A) 10
    B) 100
    C) 1,000
    D) 10,000

2) What is the sample size?

    A) 10
    B) 100
    C) 1,000
    D) 10,000

For problems 3-5 use the following situation.

A teacher wishes to know the student's opinion on the school's new attendance policy. There are 600 students in the school evenly fitting into 30 classes, and knowing that she cannot have the whole school surveyed she decides to randomly pick 4 of the classes, and survey each of the students in them.

3) What is the population size?

    A) 20
    B) 80
    C) 100
    D) 600

4) What is the sample size?

   A) 20
   B) 80
   C) 100
   D) 500

5) What type of sample did the teacher conduct?

   A) Cluster Sample
   B) Stratified Random Sample
   C) Convenience Sample
   D) Simple Random Sample

For questions 6-7 use the following situation.

A researcher wishes to determine if effects of ingesting chemical A include death. He tests a certain group of 300 mice. He puts all of the mice on the same sleeping, eating, and exercise schedule. However, he administers varying amounts of the chemical to different groups of mice, and records the number of mice to die within a month.

6) What is the explanatory variable?

   A) Number of mice is the study
   B) How much sleep the mice get
   C) Amount of chemical A ingested
   D) Number of mice dead

7) What is the response variable?

   A) Number of mice is the study
   B) How much sleep the mice get
   C) Amount of chemical A ingested
   D) Number of mice dead

8) For the diagram below, what is most likely represented by lines A and B respectively?

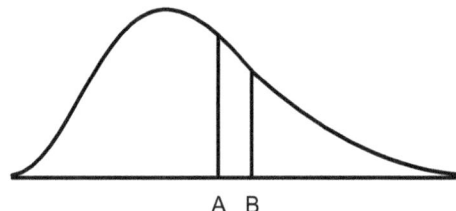

A) Median, Mean
B) Mean, Median
C) Mode, Mean
D) Median, Mode

9) Which of the following is a scatterplot?

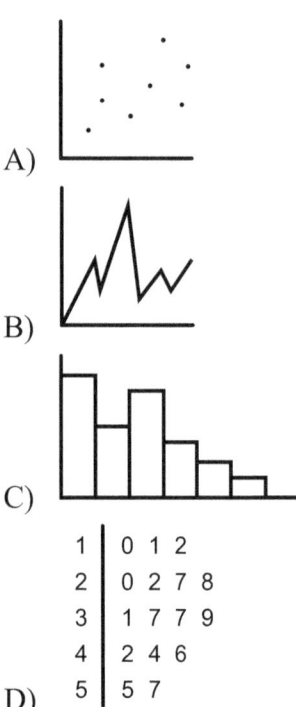

10) What type of graph is pictured below?

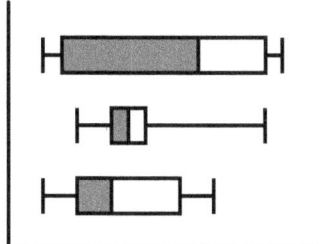

A) Box plot
B) Scatterplot
C) Histogram
D) Stem and Leaf plot

11) Which of the following terms does NOT relate to sampling methods?

A) Simple Random Sample
B) Block Design
C) Cluster Sample
D) All of the above relate to sampling methods

12) What is the median of the following stem and leaf plot?

```
6 | 0 1
5 | 1 3 6
4 | 3 4 4 6 8 9
3 | 0 1 2 4
2 | 3 4
1 | 4
0 | 1
```

A) 44
B) 46
C) 48
D) 49
E) 39.15

13) Which of the following data sets has the highest standard deviation?

X={1, 1, 2, 3, 4, 5}
Y={1, 2, 3, 4, 5}
Z={4, 5, 6, 7, 8}

A) X
B) Y
C) Z
D) Both Y and Z are equally high

14) Which of the following data sets has the highest standard deviation?

A= {1, 2, 5, 9, 10}
B= {1, 1, 2, 2, 3, 7, 9}
C= { 7, 7, 7, 8, 8, 9, 10}

A) A
B) B
C) C
D) A and B are equally high
E) B and C are equally high

15) Which of the following data sets have the smallest and largest mean respectively?

A= {1, 2, 5, 9, 10}
B= {1, 1, 2, 2, 3, 7, 9}
C= { 7, 7, 7, 8, 8, 9, 10}

A) A, B
B) A, C
C) B, A
D) B, C
E) C, B

16) Which of the following sets of data has the smallest mean?

R={7, 7, 7, 8, 8, 9}
S={1, 2, 3, 4, 5, 6, 7, 8, 9}
T={4, 4, 5, 5, 6, 6, 7}

A) R
B) S
C) T
D) Cannot be determined

For questions 17-18 use the following situation.

Jim, a high school senior, wishes to know how many students his age listen to music while studying. To find out he devises a survey, and distributes it to all of the students in one of his class periods. He then analyzes the data and comes to a conclusion.

17) What is the population of the student's survey?

A) All of the students in the school.
B) The students in the surveyed classes.
C) All of the seniors in the school.
D) The seniors and teachers in the school.

18) Which of the following best describe the student's survey?

A) Stratified random sample
B) Simple random sample
C) Cluster sample
D) Convenience sample

19) A scientist develops a new type of medication and wishes to test it. In order to do this he randomly divides the subjects into a control group and an experimental group. He has assistants administer the medication to half of the subjects, and a placebo to the other half. The subjects do not know which they are receiving, and those determining the effectiveness do not know which drug each patient is receiving either. Which of the following best describe his experiment?

A) Double blind experiment
B) Matched pairs design
C) Block design
D) Placebo effect

20) A footwear company has just designed a new type of running shoes and wishes to test their durability. They randomly distribute 1000 pairs of the new shoe to be tested. In order to get more comprehensive results they divide the shoes among people who are regular runners and people who are not. Which of the following best describes the experiment?

A) Matched pairs design
B) Double blind experiment
C) Block design
D) Placebo effect

Probability (15)

For problems 1-3 use the following table.

Card:	1	2	3	5	7	9
Probability:	.1	.1	.3	.1	?	.1

1) What is the probability of drawing a 7?

A) .1
B) .2
C) .3
D) .5

2) What is the mean number of card drawn?

A) 3.9
B) 4.5
C) 5
D) 6.1

3) Assuming that an even number must be drawn, what is the probability of winning?

A) 0
B) .1
C) .5
D) 1

4) If P(A)=.4 and P(B)=.2, then assuming that the two events are independent and disjoint what are the probabilities of $P(A \cup B)$ and $P(A \cap B)$ respectively?

   A) .2 and .08
   B) .6 and .08
   C) .08 and .6
   D) Not possible

5) Given that P(C)=.5, P(D)=.6 and the fact that the two events are independent, what is $P(C \cup D)$

   A) .3
   B) .7
   C) .8
   D) 1.1

6) Evaluate $P(B|A)$ if P(A)=.3, P(B)=.4 and the two events are independent.

   A) .3
   B) .4
   C) .5
   D) Cannot be determined

7) The numbers 1-6 are written on papers and put in a bag. If you take two out at a time, and don't replace numbers in between, how many possible arrangements of the numbers are there?

   A) 60
   B) 50
   C) 40
   D) 30

8) A drawer contains one quarter, one dime, one nickel and one penny. Drawing three at a time, how many different amounts could you possibly draw out of the drawer?

   A) $\dfrac{4!}{1!}$

   B) $\dfrac{4!}{3!(1)!}$

   C) $\dfrac{3!}{(4)!}$

   D) $\dfrac{3!}{4!(1)!}$

9) A bag of marbles contains 10 marbles. If you decide to randomly give 3 to your friend, how many possible combinations of marbles could your friend receive?

   A) $_{10}C_3$
   B) $_{10}P_3$
   C) $_3C_{10}$
   D) $_3P_{10}$

10) Considering a fair die, what is the probability of rolling a five?

   A) $\dfrac{5}{6}$

   B) $\dfrac{1}{5}$

   C) $\dfrac{1}{6}$

   D) $\dfrac{1}{2}$

11) Consider a standard deck of 52 playing cards. What is the probability of drawing a heart or an ace?

   A) $\frac{16}{52}$

   B) $\frac{1}{4}$

   C) $\frac{14}{52}$

   D) $\frac{17}{52}$

12) Consider a standard deck of 52 playing cards. What is the probability of drawing a king or a queen?

   A) $\frac{15}{52}$

   B) $\frac{3}{16}$

   C) $\frac{5}{13}$

   D) $\frac{2}{13}$

13) If a variable follows a Normal distribution, what is the probability that a value will be within one standard deviation of the mean?

   A) 25%
   B) 65%
   C) 74%
   D) 95%

14) If a continuous random variable follows a uniform distribution what is the probability that $.2 \leq x \leq .5$?

    A) .3
    B) .4
    C) .5
    D) .6

15) Which of the following is NOT a discrete random variable?

    A) A spinner divided into 50 different sections.
    B) A spinner for which the whole circle is labeled A.
    C) A spinner divided into three portions labeled A, B, and C.
    D) All of the above are discrete random variables.

Correlation and Regression (20)

1) Which of the following best describes the correlation of the following graph?

    A) Weakly positive
    B) Weakly negative
    C) Strongly positive
    D) Strongly negative

2) Which of the following best describes the correlation of the following graph?

    A) Weakly negative
    B) Strongly positive
    C) Strongly negative
    D) No correlation

3) Which of the following best describes the correlation of the following graph?

A) Weakly positive
B) Weakly negative
C) Strongly positive
D) No correlation

4) Which of the following has the weakest correlation?

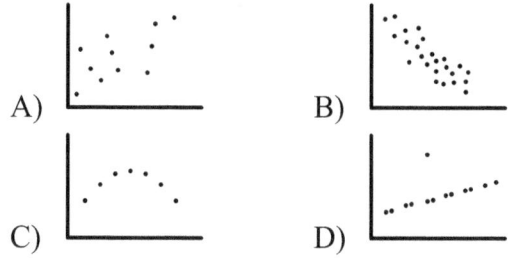

5) Which of the following has the strongest correlation?

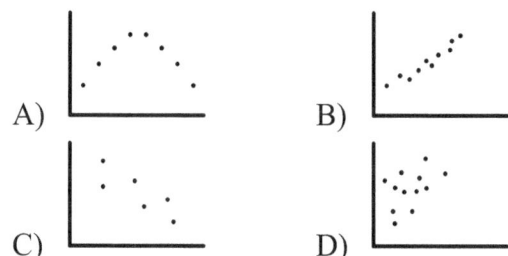

For problems 6-12 use the following data set.

X:	16	24	29	35	48	50
Y:	12	18	21	26	33	40

6) Determine $\bar{y}$

   A) 33.67
   B) 35
   C) 31.14
   D) 25

7) Determine $\bar{x}$

   A) 33.67
   B) 35
   C) 31.14
   D) 25

8) Determine s_x

   A) 11.4
   B) 9.3
   C) 12.3
   D) 8.26

9) Determine s_y

   A) 16.4
   B) 12.3
   C) 9.3
   D) 8.26

10) Determine r

    A) .59
    B) .44
    C) .89
    D) .64

11) Determine the coefficient of determination

   A) .35
   B) .19
   C) .79
   D) .41

12) Determine the line of best fit for the data set

   A) $\hat{y} = .351x + 13.8$
   B) $\hat{y} = .423x + 12.2$
   C) $\hat{y} = .985x + 5.21$
   D) $\hat{y} = .388x + 14.3$

13) If a data set has correlation $r = .899$ and standard deviations such that $s_y = 24$ and $s_x = 6$, and assuming when x is zero y is zero, what is the line of best fit for the data?

   A) $\hat{y} = .899x + 4$
   B) $\hat{y} = 4x + .889$
   C) $\hat{y} = .36x$
   D) $\hat{y} = .36x + 4$

14) Which of the following most correctly fits a line of best fit to its data?

   A)    B)

   C) 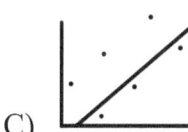   D)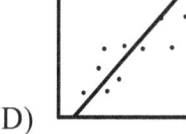

15) Determine the correlation of the following data set

X:	1	3	2	9	7
Y:	22	65	66	48	59

A) .19
B) .2
C) .36
D) .40

16) Determine the correlation of the following data set

X:	32	35	38	39	42
Y:	102	113	125	140	156

A) .79
B) .77
C) .89
D) .99

17) Which of the following best describes extrapolation?

A) Attempting to use a line of best fit to estimate a value which outside the range of the data.
B) Using the data to predict specific values within the known range of data.
C) Analyzing the data to come to conclusions about the population which it describes.
D) None of the above correctly describes extrapolation.

18) A data set follows the equation such that $\hat{y} = 1.336x + 2$. If $r = .65$ and $s_x = 3.46$ then what is the standard deviation of the y values?

A) 6.8
B) 7.1
C) 7.5
D) 8.2

19) A data set follows the equation such that $\hat{y} = 2.94x + 5$. If $s_x = 1.2$ and $s_y = 3.6$, then what is the correlation of the data?

   A) 1
   B) .98
   C) .89
   D) .77

20) If the coefficient of determination is equal to .25, what is the correlation of the data?

   A) .25
   B) .35
   C) .5
   D) .99

Sampling Distributions (20)

For questions 1-4 use the following information

An astrology class has just taken their first test. The teacher is interested to see how the class did, and decides to create a histogram of their scores. He discovers that the scores for the class follow a Normal distribution, with the mean score being 75 correct out of 100 questions. The standard deviation of the scores is 13.

1) Approximately what percentage of the students scored 90 or more questions correct?

   A) 15%
   B) 12.5%
   C) 87.5%
   D) 60%

2) Approximately what percentage of the students scored 50 or fewer questions correct?

   A) 6.2%
   B) 12.5%
   C) 45.3%
   D) 61.2%

3) What score describes the 80th percentile for this test?

   A) 95
   B) 89
   C) 86
   D) 80

4) If you randomly selected a student from the class, what is the probability that they answered 45 or more questions correctly?

   A) .65
   B) .99
   C) .01
   D) .54

For problems 5-7 use the following scenario

A refrigerator company routinely checks random refrigerators for dents to be sure they are producing high quality merchandise. On a certain day 120 refrigerators are pulled to be checked. The mean number of dents for the sample is $\bar{x} = 1.2$. Assume that standard deviation of dents in refrigerators for the company is .8.

5) What is the mean number of dents for all of the refrigerators manufactured by the company?

   A) .8
   B) 1.5
   C) 2
   D) 1.2

6) What is the standard deviation of dents in the sample of refrigerators taken?

   A) .07
   B) .5
   C) .6
   D) 1.2

7) Assuming that the number of dents follows a Normal distribution, what percentage of refrigerators have more than 3 dents?

   A) 1%
   B) 3%
   C) 5%
   D) 12%

For problems 8-12 use the following situation

There are 15,000 high school students in a specific district who watch a specific television show. The proportion of students who watch the show is $p = .36$. 1500 students are randomly polled and asked whether or not they watch the television show.

8) What is the mean proportion of students who watch the show for the sampling distribution?

   A) .33
   B) .34
   C) .35
   D) .36

9) What is the standard deviation of the sampling distribution?

   A) .012
   B) .021
   C) .312
   D) .224

10) What is the probability that a random sample will have $\hat{p} \le .34$?

    A) .0016
    B) .0475
    C) .0262
    D) .2643

11) What is the probability that a random sample will have $\hat{p} \ge .51$?

    A) Less than .0001
    B) .0014
    C) .1056
    D) .0510

12) If a 150 person sample was used instead, what would the standard deviation be?

   A) .001
   B) .027
   C) .039
   D) .34

For questions 13 and 14 use the following information

A sampling distribution of size n=25 follows an approximately Normal distribution, and has $\mu_{\bar{x}} = 2$. The standard deviation of the population is $\sigma = .35$.

13) What is the mean of the population?

   A) 1
   B) 2
   C) 3
   D) 4

14) What is the standard deviation of the sampling distribution?

   A) .4
   B) .56
   C) .7
   D) 1.2

15) Under what conditions may the sampling distribution of $\hat{p}$ be assumed Normal?

   I. $np \geq 10$
   II. $n(1-p) \geq 10$
   III. $N \geq 10n$

   A) III only
   B) II and III only
   C) I, II, and III
   D) I and II only

16) Under what conditions is $\sigma_{\hat{p}} = \sqrt{\dfrac{p(1-p)}{n}}$ a valid assumption?

I. $np \geq 10$
II. $n(1-p) \geq 10$
III. $N \geq 10n$

A) III only
B) II and III only
C) I, II, and III
D) I and II only

For questions 17-20 use the following four graphs of sampling distributions

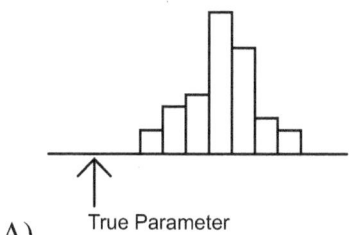
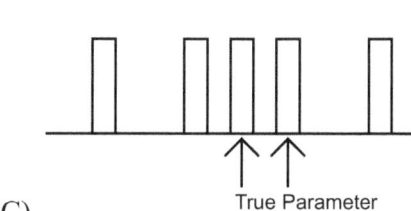

17) Which of the graphs best demonstrates low bias and low variability?

A) A
B) B
C) C
D) D

18) Which of the graphs best demonstrates low bias and high variability?

A) A
B) B
C) C
D) D

19) Which of the graphs best demonstrates high bias and high variability?

   A) A
   B) B
   C) C
   D) D

20) Which of the graphs best demonstrates high bias and low variability?

   A) A
   B) B
   C) C
   D) D

Inferential Statistics (25)

For problems 1-4 use the following information

A construction worker wishes to know the average number of months it takes to build a home. To determine this he follows a random sample of 100 homes as they are being built, and records the number of months it takes to finish them. He determines that $\bar{x} = 4.3$. Assume that the known standard deviation for building time is $\sigma = 2.6$.

1) What is the value z^* for the data assuming an 80% confidence interval?

   A) 1.17
   B) 1.28
   C) -1.18
   D) 1.78

2) What is the value for z^* for the data assuming a 99% confidence interval?

   A) 2.585
   B) 1.245
   C) 1.879
   D) 2.575

3) Which of the following is a correct 80% confidence interval for the data?

   A) (3.97, 4.63)
   B) (3.86, 4.54)
   C) (3.63, 4.97)
   D) (4.01, 5.02)

4) Which of the following is a correct 99% confidence interval for the data?

   A) (3.97, 4.63)
   B) (3.63, 4.97)
   C) (3.86, 4.54)
   D) (4.01, 5.02)

For problems 5-8 use the following table

3	4	8	4	6
5	9	1	5	4
8	6	2	9	7
6	5	1	3	0
5	1	3	0	8
1	6	8	4	5

5) What is the value t* for the data used in a 99.9% confidence interval?

   A) 3.745
   B) 3.291
   C) 3.675
   D) 3.232

6) Which of the following is the correct 99.9% confidence interval for the data?

   A) (3.1, 7.4)
   B) (4.23, 4.91)
   C) (2.9, 6.6)
   D) (4.32, 4.91)

7) What is the value t* for the data used in a 50% confidence interval?

   A) .156
   B) .855
   C) .685
   D) .681

8) Which of the following is the correct 50% confidence interval for the data?

   A) (3.1, 7.4)
   B) (4.32, 4.91)
   C) (4.23, 4.91)
   D) (2.9, 6.6)

9) Which of the following can be concluded from a 95% confidence interval?

I. The probability that the mean is within the interval is .95
II. The method used in constructing the interval is correct 95% of the time
III. There is a 5% chance that the interval is incorrect

   A) I and III only
   B) II only
   C) II and I only
   D) None of the statements are correct

10) What is a type I error?

   A) Accepting a hypothesis which should have been rejected.
   B) Accepting a hypothesis which should have been accepted.
   C) Rejecting a hypothesis which should have been rejected.
   D) Rejecting a hypothesis which should have been accepted.

11) What is a type II error?

   A) Accepting a hypothesis which should have been rejected.
   B) Accepting a hypothesis which should have been accepted.
   C) Rejecting a hypothesis which should have been rejected.
   D) Rejecting a hypothesis which should have been accepted.

12) If a 99% confidence interval is constructed, what is the chance of making a Type I error?

   A) .99
   B) .05
   C) .45
   D) .67

13) If an 80% confidence interval is constructed, what is the chance of making a Type I error?

   A) .2
   B) .8
   C) .46
   D) .85

14) When is a t score used in place of a z score?

   A) Whenever a confidence interval is being constructed.
   B) When the sample size is very small, or when the sample size is at most 25.
   C) When the standard deviation for the population is not known.
   D) None of the above

15) Determine the standard error of a 21 person study for which $s = 34$

   A) 3.60
   B) 4.51
   C) 6.86
   D) 7.42

16) If standard error is 9.65, and there were 20 people in a study, then what is the standard deviation of the sample?

   A) 40.1
   B) 42.5
   C) 62.8
   D) Cannot be determined without knowing the standard deviation of the population

17) What is the margin of error if $\sigma = .264$, $n = 1500$, and the confidence level is 99.9%?

   A) .0156
   B) .022
   C) 1.26
   D) 3.28

18) Which of the following symbols indicates a critical value?

   A) t*
   B) z*
   C) z^c
   D) $\bar{x}$

For problems 19-22 use the following table of information

	Parameters			Statistics		
	Population Size	Mean	Standard Deviation	Sample Size	Mean	Standard deviation
Set 1:	1000	3.57	.95	95	3.68	.86
Set 2:	1500	4.14	.84	150	3.99	.39

19) Determine the variance of the two samples

   A) .051
   B) .015
   C) .002
   D) .001

20) Determine the two sample z statistic

   A) 7.01
   B) 2.01
   C) .52
   D) 1.12

21) What is $\bar{x}_2^2$?

   A) .15
   B) .74
   C) .9
   D) .71

22) What is σ_2^2?

   A) .15
   B) .74
   C) .9
   D) .71

For problems 23-25 use the following situation

A hospital director wishes to know how long it takes the on call employees to report for duty. One year all of the times are recorded and it is determined that the average arrival time for all on call employees fits a Normal distribution with $\mu = 10.2$ minutes and $\sigma = 3.5$ minutes. The director informs the employees that for the next year she wants the average report time to be under ten minutes. At the end of the next year she takes a random sample of 200 report times. The sample yields $\bar{x} = 9.7$ minutes. Assuming the standard deviation has not changed from the previous year, she feels that there is a good chance that the actual times have not changed, and that the sample is not an accurate representation of the data.

23) What is the null hypothesis for the data?

   A) $Y_0 : \mu < 10.2$
   B) $Y_0 : \mu > 10.2$
   C) $Y_0 : \mu = 10.2$
   D) $Y_0 : \mu \neq 10.2$

24) What is the z statistic for the data?

   A) 3.65
   B) 2.02
   C) -2.02
   D) -3.65

25) Has the average report time really decreased?

   A) It is likely that the average report time has increased because the z statistic is so low.
   B) It is likely that the average report time has decreased because the z statistic is so low.
   C) It is likely that the average report time has increased because the z statistic is so high.
   D) It is likely that the average report time has decreased because the z statistic is so high.

Answer Key

Foundations of Statistics	Probability	Correlation and Regression	Sampling Distributions	Inferential Statistics
1. D	1. C	1. A	1. B	1. B
2. B	2. A	2. C	2. A	2. D
3. D	3. B	3. D	3. C	3. A
4. B	4. D	4. C	4. B	4. B
5. A	5. C	5. B	5. D	5. A
6. C	6. B	6. D	6. A	6. C
7. D	7. D	7. A	7. D	7. C
8. A	8. B	8. C	8. D	8. C
9. A	9. A	9. C	9. A	9. D
10. A	10. C	10. B	10. B	10. D
11. B	11. A	11. B	11. A	11. A
12. C	12. D	12. A	12. C	12. B
13. D	13. B	13. C	13. B	13. A
14. A	14. A	14. D	14. C	14. C
15. B	15. D	15. B	15. D	15. D
16. B		16. D	16. A	16. B
17. C		17. A	17. D	17. B
18. D		18. B	18. C	18. B
19. A		19. B	19. B	19. D
20. C		20. C	20. A	20. A
				21. A
				22. D
				23. C
				24. C
				25. B

 Test Taking Strategies

Here are some test-taking strategies that are specific to this test and to other DSST tests in general:

- Keep your eyes on the time. Pay attention to how much time you have left.

- Read the entire question and read all the answers. Many questions are not as hard to answer as they may seem. Sometimes, a difficult sounding question really only is asking you how to read an accompanying chart. Chart and graph questions are on most DANTES/DSST tests and should be an easy free point.

- If you don't know the answer immediately, the new computer-based testing lets you mark questions and come back to them later if you have time.

- Read the wording carefully. Some words can give you hints to the right answer. There are no exceptions to an answer when there are words in the question such as always, all or none. If one of the answer choices includes most or some of the right answers, but not all, then that is not the answer. Here is an example:

    The primary colors include all of the following:

    A) Red, Yellow, Blue, Green

    B) Red, Green, Yellow

    C) Red, Orange, Yellow

    D) Red, Yellow, Blue

    Although item A includes all the right answers, it also includes an incorrect answer, making it incorrect. If you didn't read it carefully, were in a hurry, or didn't know the material well, you might fall for this.

- Make a guess on a question that you do not know the answer to. There is no penalty for an incorrect answer. Eliminate the answer choices that you know are incorrect. For example, this will let your guess be a 1 in 3 chance instead.

Legal Note

All rights reserved. This Study Guide, Book and Flashcards are protected under US Copyright Law. No part of this book or study guide or flashcards may be reproduced, distributed or stored in a retrieval system, or transmitted in any form or by any means, electronic, mechanical, photocopying, recording, or otherwise, without the prior written permission of the publisher Breely Crush Publishing, LLC.

DSST is a registered trademark of The Thomson Corporation and its affiliated companies, and does not endorse this book.

FLASHCARDS

This section contains flashcards for you to use to further your understanding of the material and test yourself on important concepts, names or dates. Read the term or question then flip the page over to check the answer on the back. Keep in mind that this information may not be covered in the text of the study guide. Take your time to study the flashcards, you will need to know and understand these concepts to pass the test.

Mode	Median
Mean	Permutation
Probability	Upper quartile
Lower quartile	Normal approximation for data

The middle value	The number that appears most number of times in the sample data
An ordered sequence of items taken from a set without replacement	Sum of all values, then divided by the number of values present
A number such that at least 75% of the numbers in the data set are no larger than this number	The likelihood an event will occur as expressed by ratios
Data in a histogram based on the normal curve if the data values are converted to standards units	A number such that at least 25% of the numbers in the dataset are no larger than this number

Standard deviation	In standard deviation, the N stands for
Correlation	Regression
Estimated variable	Linear correlation
What is a scatter diagram?	If r = 0 then

Number of values in the data set	Data points to the mean of the sample data set
An estimation of one variable based on one or more related variables	Which variables satisfy an equation or criteria in a situation
When all points on a scatter diagram appear to lie close to a line	Dependent variable
There is no correlation between the variables	Displays the locations and relationships of two variables (X,Y) on a rectangular coordinate system

If r = 1 then	In linear regression, x is for
In linear regression, y is for	Conditional probability
Dependent events	Can mutually exclusive events happen at the same time?
Combinations	Sampling theory

Independent variable	There is a perfect correlation between the variables
Conditional probability looks at the probability that more than one event occurs	Dependent variable
No	An event is dependent if the outcome of one event depends on the outcome of the other event
The study of relationships between a population and samples taken from the population	An unordered subset of items taken from a group of distinct items

Random sampling	**Confidence level**
Null hypothesis	**Type I error**
Type II error	**Inductive statistics**
Descriptive statistics	**Domain**

Refers to the percentage confidence	When each member of a population has an equal chance of being included in the sample
When you reject a hypothesis that should have been accepted	A statement which you wish to test
Statistics that enable you to make conclusions and decisions based on data	When you accept a hypothesis when it should have been rejected
All the possible values you can use "x" for in the function of the ordered pair	Meant to describe and analyze a group without making a decision

Ordered Pair	Another name for empty set
Class interval	Size interval
Class mark	Second quartile
Z score	Positive linear correlation

Null set	(x,y)
Determined by finding the difference between the upper and lower limit for the category	The upper and lower limit for each category
Median	Located at the midpoint of the class interval
Y tends to increase as X increases	A mean score divided by the standard deviation

NOTES

NOTES

NOTES

NOTES

NOTES

NOTES

NOTES

NOTES

NOTES

NOTES

NOTES

NOTES

NOTES

NOTES

NOTES

NOTES

NOTES

NOTES

NOTES

NOTES

NOTES

NOTES

NOTES

NOTES

NOTES

NOTES

NOTES

NOTES

NOTES

NOTES

NOTES

NOTES

NOTES

NOTES

NOTES

NOTES

NOTES

NOTES

NOTES

NOTES

NOTES

NOTES

NOTES

NOTES

www.ingramcontent.com/pod-product-compliance
Lightning Source LLC
Chambersburg PA
CBHW081831300426
44116CB00014B/2553